Tea Party
Patriots

Tea Party Patriots

THE SECOND AMERICAN REVOLUTION

MARK MECKLER

AND

JENNY BETH MARTIN

HENRY HOLT AND COMPANY

NEW YORK

Henry Holt and Company, LLC
Publishers since 1866
175 Fifth Avenue
New York, New York 10010

Henry Holt® is a registered trademark of Henry Holt and Company, LLC.

Library of Congress Cataloging-in-Publication Data

Meckler, Mark.
 Tea Party Patriots : the second American revolution / Mark Meckler and
Jenny Beth Martin.—1st ed.
     p. cm.
 Includes bibliographical references and index.
 ISBN 978-0-8050-9437-4
 1. Tea Party Patriots.   2. Tea Party movement.   I. Martin, Jenny Beth.
II. Title.
 JK2391.T43M43 2012
 320.520973—dc23   2011039380

Henry Holt books are available for special promotions and premiums.
For details contact: Director, Special Markets.

First Edition 2012
Designed by Meryl Sussman Levavi
Printed in the United States of America
               1   3   5   7   9   10   8   6   4   2

To all of America's patriots:
past, present, and future

Contents

Tea Party
Patriots

Introduction

Jenny Beth Martin

IN EARLY 2009, as I was cleaning one of my neighbors' houses, a job I had taken to support my young family, there were a few things I *never* would have imagined would happen to me. If someone had told me then that I would soon be writing a book about American politics, I would have laughed. And if someone had said that just one year later, I would be named one of the one hundred most influential people in the world by *Time* magazine, I probably would have just shaken my head and gone back to dusting.

I did not feel influential on that cool February morning. I felt like a graying mother of young twins who had just lost her Atlanta family home to foreclosure. In that loss my husband, Lee, and I were not alone. Millions of Americans had lost their homes too, in what was called the worst foreclosure crisis in American history. Millions more, like us, had also found themselves newly out of work, with the U.S. unemployment rate climbing to levels not seen since the Great Depression.

Yes, our house was big and beautiful. More house than we needed. But it wasn't more house than we could afford when we signed our mortgage. Lee ran a successful temporary staffing business. I worked part-time. We bought that house the same way our parents bought theirs: with a big down payment, credit checks at the bank, and monthly payments that were within our means.

But then the ground fell out from under us. Lee's business began to struggle and ultimately he lost the business. I lost a child by miscarriage. And we lost our home.

America was in crisis. Markets were melting down. Jobs were evaporating. And fears were springing up that America—and the world's economy—might not survive.

Lee and I were not alone in our moment of crisis, but we felt that way. We certainly weren't aligned with what the politicians in Washington, D.C., were saying. It seemed that the government of our country was promoting the idea that everyone *deserved* a bailout when they got in financial trouble. We didn't think we deserved a bailout. Like most Americans, we believed in taking responsibility for our own situation in life.

When Lee's business collapsed, we did not look to the government for a bailout. We looked to each other and to our faith in God for strength. We could have easily taken a Washington handout. There were billions of bailout dollars flying around the country. Our bank actually offered us a new, government-guaranteed loan to bring us current on our house payments and allow us to avoid losing our home. But, as Lee said, and I agreed, "It is not right for our neighbors to pay for our house." And so we started over.

We began a small business with a payroll of two: Lee and me. We went from owning a large company with thousands of employees to being small entrepreneurs again. We knew what it took to succeed: hard work, integrity, and ethics. We'd done it before, and we were confident in our own ability to provide for our family. And we weren't too proud to do whatever it took. We looked around, saw a need, and decided to provide a valuable service to our neighbors—we cleaned their houses. It was hard but honest work, and it certainly wasn't beneath us, no matter what we had done before.

Lee and I had been raised to respect the value of hard work and self-reliance. We grew up in a country where, if you applied yourself and worked hard, you could live the American dream. We were living that dream before it turned into a nightmare. But we never lost our faith that America is the land of opportunity: the best place in the world to go broke and start over.

And so we did. Our "head office" was our car. Inside our car was a radio. And it was on that radio—as we drove from one house to the next on February 19, 2009—that we heard the words that would change our lives forever.

> *This is America! How many of you people want to pay for your neighbor's mortgages [when they have] an extra bathroom and can't pay their bills?*

The contrast hit me hard. While my husband and I cleaned our neighbors' bathrooms to pay our bills, our taxes were being spent by our government to pay for the mortgages of people who could not, or would not, pay *their* bills.

The speaker on the radio was CNBC reporter Rick Santelli, on the floor of the Chicago Mercantile Exchange, in his now-famous rant that sparked the modern Tea Party movement. "We're thinking of having a Chicago Tea Party in July," he said. "All you Capitalists that want to show up at Lake Michigan, I'm gonna start organizing."

The next day, I started organizing, too. But I had little idea where to begin.

I had never organized a protest before. I had never even *been* to a protest. But I had been active online. And I did understand politics. Most important, I knew that the time had come to do something to save the country. I was reminded, deep inside, of something that Ronald Reagan said in his second inaugural address: "If not us, who? And if not now, when?" As I looked at my young children, I could not shake the thought that this was my personal responsibility as a citizen and as a mother.

Because I had been very active on Facebook, Twitter, and other social media, it was easy for me to quickly put up a Facebook page for an event in Atlanta. And I already had a political network, having been involved at the local and state levels for many years. So this was second nature to me. Immediately folks began to respond, and the Facebook page was flooded with interest from people in Atlanta who were just as fed up as I was.

A little over a week later, five hundred people showed up at the capitol in Atlanta in forty-degree weather, in a driving rain. Moms, dads, kids, and men in business suits and ties braved the weather. They held signs that universally condemned a government that they believed was not listening to them. I was inspired and overjoyed to see every one of those people. They were my first local brothers and sisters in what was to become an epic and long-term battle. The troops had arrived, and the battle was engaged.

Returning home from the event that day, I was euphoric. Even in the midst of our own personal financial problems, I knew this was a cause into which I had to throw myself completely. And my husband agreed. So we made a plan, and I began to reach out around Georgia and around the country to find out who else was involved.

In the process I met several people reaching out in the same manner, and we formed a core working group to figure out what to do next. Out of those early efforts came the idea for the Tax Day Tea Party, on April 15, 2009, an event that put the Tea Party movement on the national political map. And it was during this process that I met a newly minted activist across the country in California named Mark Meckler. Little did I know that we would go on to work together for years to come, and found and grow one of the largest grassroots political organizations in U.S. history.

MARK MECKLER

I'M A NEWS junkie. I've been using the Web to get my daily dose of information since 1993. I was fortunate in that by getting online so early, I was able to bypass the mainstream media and figure out that there were people out there who believed the things I believed, and who shared my political philosophies, despite what the *New York Times*, or CBS, or NPR might be saying to the contrary.

But prior to the Tea Party movement I was mainly an observer, not an active participant. I did have a simple Facebook page (with about ten friends), and though I was familiar with Twitter and other social networking platforms as an Internet lawyer, I had never personally used them. Offline, I sought out people who shared my vision of America; the kind of patriotism and "cowboy ethics" instilled in me by my parents, which I worked to pass down to my thirteen-year-old son and nine-year-old daughter.

Three years ago I was living the American dream: working for myself as a lawyer and entrepreneur, living rurally, happily married, and raising two fantastic kids. It had been nearly ten years since I had given up on being a Republican and had registered to vote under the party affiliation "decline to state." In disgust, I had abandoned the politicians who had themselves abandoned the values to which I held true. But I had not given up on America. I knew the real America, the America of the Founding Fathers, resided in the hearts and minds of tens of millions of Americans just like me.

As I followed political news, over the years I noted that something strange happened to politicians after they got elected. Not only did they forget about the people who sent them to Washington, they also seemed to forget about the principles that built this nation, and the oath they swore to uphold those principles. Republican or Democrat—it did not seem to matter which side was in power. Either way our government kept getting bigger, our liberties kept getting smaller, and our nation kept moving away from the ideas that made it great. The speed with which we drifted away from the founding principles ebbed and flowed, but the direction never seemed to change.

Like many Americans, I griped about the direction of the country with my friends—ranchers, loggers, contractors, real estate developers—the productive, hardworking people of our community. We even started a discussion group where a few of us could pretend to solve the country's problems over a beer or two. But beyond voting and airing my grievances with my friends, I did little to contribute to a solution.

On September 29, 2008, a Republican administration tried to pass the so-called Emergency Economic Stabilization Act, which would have turned America's founding principles upside down by rewarding extravagance and failure instead of prudence and success, while destroying a once-capitalist system that was built on the trade-off between risk and reward. It didn't matter what the government called it; everyone knew what it was: a bailout, plain and simple, for businesses that were deemed "too big to fail."

I also knew that no matter what happened to me, the government would never deem my family "too big to fail." We didn't have the political clout of big companies with highly paid lobbyists in D.C. My wife and I had two children to take care of in our modest home in Nevada County, California. Which meant we had no room to fail. And that's just how we liked it. Taking care of ourselves, standing or falling on our own efforts.

I was a lawyer by trade, but an entrepreneur by nature, and that instinct had always driven my professional life. When I got married, my wife and I moved to a small town in order to raise a family. For our economic survival, we opened a little café, and I hung out a shingle to practice law. Whatever it took to have a quality family lifestyle was key to us. Since I started my family, my main goal in life has been to spend time with my wife and kids, not to get caught up in politics, and certainly not to find myself immersed in a huge grassroots uprising.

After five years in the café business, we found that though we were doing well, the life of a restaurateur was an almost round-the-clock venture, so we sold that place and started another small business that served the ski industry, thinking it would be more of a nine-to-five type of venture. Unfortunately, that business failed due to my inexperience, and as with most Americans, no one bailed us out. The potential reward was ours, but so was the risk. We lost a lot of money and went through some tough times. But we never turned to the government for help. It's just not in our nature.

A hundred years ago, working from home probably wouldn't have been possible. I would have been stuck in some factory, or spent most of my time in an office, just to make enough money to give my family the life they deserved. But capitalism, and the technology innovation that went along with it, allowed me to make a good living working from home. I became an expert in Internet marketing law, wound up working in Internet marketing, and was involved with clients and companies around the world.

My office was right next to the kitchen, and when the kids came home from school, they would join me and do their homework. They got to see what "making a living" looked like up close, and my wife and I got to spend the maximum amount of time together and with our kids.

We got to have the maximum impact on how our kids viewed the world, and looked at every day as a teaching experience. Though the kids attended public schools, there was a lot of homeschooling going on too. The American flag flew proudly in our shared home office, right next to my favorite dusty cowboy hat and spurs.

Working at home as an online lawyer also allowed me the opportunity to indulge in my passion for online news and politics. And it accidentally put me in a perfect position to react when the Tea Party movement erupted into the American consciousness.

Many of us celebrated when the Emergency Economic Stabilization Act, or bailout bill, was initially defeated by a narrow margin. And many were sickened when the bill was fattened up with the addition of more pork to buy votes and then passed just a few days later.

On December 16, 2008, President George Bush appeared on CNN and actually said, "I've abandoned free-market principles to save the free-market system." A Republican president had openly repudiated the free-market capitalism that had been the engine of liberty and freedom in the world. My heart sank. For the first time in my life I thought the end of American prosperity, and ultimately democracy, might be at hand.

With the election of President Barack Obama, things only seemed to get worse. Promising "hope and change," the new president seemed to want to go farther down the road to economic ruin than even President Bush. The long arc of U.S. history toward a bloated and unsustainable federal government continued and actually accelerated at a blistering pace. Government involvement in the economy gained speed and size and began consuming everything in its path. Seven hundred billion dollars went to TARP (the Troubled Asset Relief Program). Billions more to buy, backstop, and bail out the biggest banks. To take over the world's biggest insurance company (AIG). To buy out Fannie Mae and Freddie Mac. Then Chrysler and General Motors. Then hundreds and hundreds more banks. It seemed that socialism in America was openly and rapidly on the march in our own time.

Then, on February 17, 2009, President Obama signed the American Recovery and Reinvestment Act, commonly referred to as the "stimulus" bill. A frustrated young woman in Seattle, Washington, Keli Carender, called it by its real name: pork. So did about a hundred other people who showed up at a "Porkulus" protest she organized in Seattle. They carried signs that read FAMILIES AGAINST PORKULUS and SAY NO TO GENERATIONAL THEFT. This was the prototype tea party. Most of us didn't realize it at the time, but the fight against a runaway government had begun.

The next day, President Obama announced his plan to bail out delinquent mortgages. That was enough to tip CNBC's Rick Santelli over the edge.

Under innocent questioning by anchors in New York, Santelli stood on the floor of the Chicago Mercantile Exchange and called for a "Tea party" in July.

> The government is promoting bad behavior! I'll tell you what, I have an idea . . . We're thinking of having a Chicago Tea Party in July. All you capitalists that want to show up to Lake Michigan, I'm gonna start organizing! I'll tell you what, if you read our founding fathers, people like Benjamin Franklin and Jefferson, what we're doing in this country now is making them roll over in their graves!

Within hours, the conservative commentator Rush Limbaugh broadcast Santelli's rant to more than 10 million people nationwide, adding, "This is the pulse of revolution, starting today! When the pulse of revolution starts, it just takes an action like this to inspire confidence in others who want to show up."

It was time to show up. The pulse of a revolution had started. The next day, the modern-day Tea Party movement began.

Santelli's rant hit the blogs and the news sites on the Web, and the video was forwarded as a link by millions. When I watched Santelli, and heard his passion, I pounded my desk and shouted out loud, "Yes!" Finally, someone who wasn't a conservative talking head was speaking sense on the air and standing up for the common working men and women of this country. I was inspired.

Jenny Beth Martin and others assembled on the first organized conference call of the movement. I wasn't plugged into social media as she was, so I didn't hear about it. But twenty-two people did, and they planned "tea parties" for the following week, on February 27, 2009. As folks started promoting those events on Facebook, I finally heard about it, and I wanted in, whatever that meant.

I discussed the idea with my wife. "Let's hold a tea party in Sacramento, at the state capitol," I told her. I asked her to watch the Santelli video and showed her a few "tea party" Facebook pages, and she was hooked. I did the same with my retired parents, and they became hooked too. It would be a family affair.

We started a Facebook page of our own for the Sacramento Tea Party and invited the few people I knew online. I started networking on the Web, calling local media, and doing everything I could think of, as an "activist" with no experience or training, to get the word out. We had no idea what would happen, and no idea if it would be just my family attending. But we were all in, going so far as to take the kids out of school to show them the First Amendment in action. If that had been it, we would have considered the event a success.

On February 27, 2009, with about twenty handmade signs in the back of our SUV, we drove down to Sacramento from the Sierra foothills. We were excited and nervous. We'd never protested or done anything like this before. We'd certainly never "organized" politically, and we had no idea what to expect. Would anyone show? Would people abuse us verbally or even physically? We were without reference points, conservative Americans embarking on a new frontier: political activism.

When we arrived, we were, in fact, the only ones there.

Six of us, one family, three generations, stood in front of a beautiful and, under the circumstances, intimidating, state capitol to protest against the government it represented. The first people to join us were representatives of the California State Highway Patrol, responsible for security at the capitol. They wanted to know if we had a permit, and we expressed our ignorance of the need. In fact, we were shocked. "You need a permit to protest? Really?"

Luckily, they took pity on us, invited us into their offices, and had us fill out the paperwork on the spot. God bless law enforcement. Coming from a family with a mom who is a retired correctional officer, we know how they serve, and as always, we appreciated them that day.

When we went back outside, we found out another 150 or so Americans had showed up that day. They were from both major political parties. They were young and old, unemployed and working. They were business owners and employees. They were on both sides of the social issues. But miraculously, they came together to speak in one voice, against a government run amok, a government that they all believed no longer had their best interests at heart. The debate had crossed the aisle, crossed the divide that politicians had used against us to consolidate their power. For the first time in my adult life, Americans of all stripes were standing together against a government out of control.

Returning home, I was inspired and began to reach out and network with other organizers. I called all over California to find out what had been tried, what had worked, and what had not. I was excited, and I wanted to learn. Suddenly I found myself in the midst of a group of passionate political activists, most of us totally inexperienced. It was intoxicating. I was realizing the magnitude of what had begun.

I started to reach beyond California. I met newly minted tea party activists from all over the country. All were equally passionate, and I ended up crossing paths with an extraordinary woman in Atlanta named Jenny Beth Martin. Together, we formed part of the core team that helped organize the next round of protests that really put the tea party on the map, the Tax Day Tea Party.

During the process of helping to coordinate and promote over 850 tea parties nationwide, Jenny Beth and I and several others worked as a team to form Tea Party Patriots as the go-forward organization for the movement. We had no idea what we had begun. We only knew that for our children, for our grandchildren, we could not stop. We had no choice.

∼

Jenny Beth and I are writing this book for a number of reasons. First, we think it's important for people to know how the Tea Party movement came into being. Misinformation of all sorts has been floating around, so we figured it was time to put something on the record that tells the real story.

Second, people need to know what the Tea Party movement is, and what it isn't. If all you know about the Tea Party is what you've heard from the mainstream media, you haven't gotten an accurate portrayal of who we are and what we're trying to do.

Third, we want everyone to know that Tea Party Patriots has a plan to restore America to its prior greatness. Until now, it's been easy to know what the Tea Party movement is against, but more difficult for people outside the movement to understand what it's *for*. After you read this book, you'll know.

One more thing. Jenny Beth and I are hardly the leaders of this amazing movement. She and I are two ordinary Americans who happen to have been around at the beginning, and like to talk about the movement to everyone we meet. We might be the ones speaking from the stage at rallies, or writing the e-mails, but the heart and the soul of the movement—the *real* leaders—are the individual patriots who come to the protests when it's cold and snowy, who have their representatives' offices on speed dial, and who refuse to quit until we take our country back.

None of this would be possible without these brave men and women. And to them, all we can say, again and again, is: thank you.

★ 1 ★

What the Tea Party Is, Our Core Values, and How It Grew So Quickly

WE THE PEOPLE. With those three words, our nation began. And with those three words, our story begins.

We, the people of the United States of America, felt threatened. We felt angry. We felt helpless as we watched our beloved nation—the greatest nation in world history—slip away.

We felt threatened because a government that once existed to protect our rights to life, liberty, and the pursuit of happiness had become the primary obstacle to the exercise of those rights. Our government had broken through its constitutional restraints, seized power over everything from our financial markets to our home loans, and aimed to go even farther, seeking control over things as large as our health-care system, and as small as the menus in school cafeterias.

We were angry at politicians from both parties who had abandoned any pretense of responsibility and spent not only all the money we would earn in our lives but all the money our children *and* grandchildren would earn in their lives.

And we felt helpless as we watched our free markets—the foundation of every American success story—warped into a system that thrived on backroom deals, bailouts, pork, and payoffs.

But most of all, we felt isolated in our belief that America was special, exceptional, a shining city upon a hill. We wondered why nobody else seemed to notice that the vision of America we had grown up with, held deep within our hearts, fought for, and promised to future generations, was so different from the America we saw around us.

It was missing from the values of the political class, who had abandoned the principles that allowed America to create more wealth and freedom than any nation the world had ever seen before.

Missing from our legislatures, where those who had sworn oaths to uphold our country's founding ideals had grown fat and happy and began to think of themselves as the masters of the people, rather than as their servants.

Missing from our classrooms, where America's faults had become required reading and its virtues footnoted or forgotten.

Missing from our culture, where yesterday's heroes—pioneers, soldiers, the creators of wealth and prosperity—had become today's villains, while those who undermined core American values were held up as role models.

Missing from our halls of justice, where those we count on to be guardians of the rule of law abused their power, ignored the will of the people, and gave legitimacy to those who sought to undermine our fundamental rights.

A century and a half after Abraham Lincoln resolved that "this nation, under God, shall have a new birth of freedom—and that government of the people, by the people, for the people, shall not perish from the earth," a newly elected president, who falsely wrapped himself in Lincoln's legacy, threatened to turn the American dream into an American nightmare by governing against the will of the majority, eroding America's prosperity, apologizing for America's greatness, and dimming the lights on this shining city upon a hill that had stood as a beacon of freedom, prosperity, and opportunity to the world since its founding.

Threatened, angry, helpless, and alone, we wondered why no one else seemed to share our feelings. Why did America seem like a "sleeping giant"?

Then one man, Rick Santelli, spoke out. From his heart. Without fear. Without a plan. With no idea what his words would unleash. His words spread across the country. Millions of Americans heard his call: a call for a new American Tea Party.

And the sleeping giant woke up.

∾

This book is the story of the beginning of the second American Revolution; a revolution that is being fought every day across this country not with muskets and rifles but with laptops and telephones. Its soldiers are an army of 20 million everyday Americans who are every bit as patriotic as those who gave their lives at Lexington and Concord to ensure that all of us could enjoy our God-given rights to life, liberty, and the pursuit of happiness.

It is a call to arms for those who remember how great America once was to stop what they're doing, pay attention, and join the movement that will ultimately restore America to its place as the greatest country the world has ever seen.

This is the story of all of us. This is what we need to do to take our country back.

∾

At any other time in American history, it is entirely possible—even probable—that the Tea Party movement would not have happened at all.

As inspired as people were by Santelli, and as devoted as Rush Limbaugh's listeners have always been, radio and television are primarily one-way media. Those of us who saw the rant in our living rooms, or heard the broadcast in our cars, knew one thing: there was at least one other person in the world who believed the same things we did. What we didn't know at that time was that there were tens of millions of other people in the country who felt the same way. And thanks to a technology that was less than three years old, we would very quickly find out.

When Twitter was launched in 2006, nobody could have imagined that it would soon be at the forefront of the most important American political movement of the twenty-first century. But without Twitter, those of us who had heard Santelli's rant and agreed that it was time for a change might never have been able to come together to take action. The first American Revolution may have begun with a gunshot, but the second American Revolution began with a hashtag.

Hashtags—symbols that look like this: #—are the way people self-organize into groups on Twitter. At the time of Rick Santelli's rant, the most important hashtag for what was to become the Tea Party movement was #TCOT. TCOT, which stood for "Top Conservatives On Twitter," was a short and easy acronym people could type at the end of tweets to help those who believed in America's founding principles to easily find each other online.

Less than six months earlier, in November 2008, a group of people who were dismayed at the direction in which the country was heading had already come together under the #TCOT banner to express their thoughts about what was going wrong with America and how we should fix it. About that same time, a group of conservative women who were discouraged that conservative women did not seem to want to run for elected office, and by the lack of an online organization dedicated to conservative women, came together to start Smart Girl Politics. They tweeted under the banner #SGP to begin finding ways to communicate online and educating conservative women on how to run for office and become more politically active.

As fiscal conservatives, we were appalled by the big spending policies of President George W. Bush and the Democratic Congress, and needed to talk about it with those who shared our values. And when bad government policies led to a near economic collapse in September 2008, we tweeted to express our dismay at Washington's response: propping up Fannie Mae and Freddie Mac; using taxpayer dollars to buy up mortgage-backed securities; bailing out AIG; debasing the value of the dollar; and trying to pass a "bailout" plan that rewarded bad behavior with billions of our taxpayer dollars.

By the time the stimulus was passed, the #TCOT community on Twitter had just about reached critical mass. It was a pile of kindling waiting for the spark that would ignite a national brush fire.

On the same day as Limbaugh's broadcast of Santelli's rant, Michael Patrick Leahy, who along with Rob Neppell had founded the #TCOT group, contacted the founders of Smart Girl Politics, Stacy Mott and Teri Christoph, and the founder of #DontGo, Eric Odom, to ask them if they wanted to do a conference call about the Santelli rant. After conferring with Smart Girl Politics and #DontGo, Michael Patrick Leahy tweeted an invitation to join a free conference call the next night to talk about what we could do. There were twenty-two patriots on that first conference call, held at 8:00 PM ET on Friday, February 20. It was the first time many of these people had even heard each other's voices. They had passion but no expertise.

Even now, with more than 3,500 affiliated state and local Tea Party groups who have members in the tens of millions, whatever "expertise" we have comes from the skills, time, and passion volunteered by individual Tea Party Patriots. Back in 2009, all we had was the heartfelt belief that America's founding principles were worth fighting for and that, unless *we* did something about it quickly, we risked losing everything America had become.

It was up to us to show up and take action before the other side could douse the fire in our hearts. Like our forefathers, we pledged our lives, our fortunes, and our sacred honor for America—to stand up to a government that had grown power-hungry and out of control. But we had no idea how to hold a "tea party." So we made it up as we went along.

Is this how revolutions get started? Was this how the original Sons of Liberty felt on December 16, 1773? When they tipped those 340 cases of tea into Boston Harbor, did they know they were also tipping the scales of power away from a distant, unresponsive, arrogant, corrupt government toward the people, where it belonged? Did they suspect that within eighteen months of that first tea party, the colonies would be united in war against Great Britain, and that the world would never be the same again?

We were just ordinary citizens with kids to feed and bills to pay in the middle of a collapsing economy, with Washington and our state governments trying to take more away from us each year to waste and spend or give to their cronies. Dawn Wildman, from San Diego, was a paralegal and real estate property manager. Sally Oljar was a graphic artist in Seattle. Amy Kremer was a flight attendant from

Roswell, Georgia. Debbie Dooley was a technology security specialist from Atlanta, Georgia. Those were the kinds of people present at the beginning of the movement, not high-priced spin doctors.

Our detractors have accused us of being tools of the political establishment. They suggest that everything we have done has been planned from some back room in Washington, D.C. It is only natural that they would suspect this, because that is the way *their* movements operate. They cannot imagine or accept the truth: that we are a true grassroots movement of citizens who joined together to defend America against politicians who swore to uphold the Constitution, but who instead fed it through a shredder along with trillions of our taxpayer dollars. Our detractors cannot accept that we are who we are, because it threatens their warped worldview. And so they convince themselves (and few others) that we are an "Astroturf" group; that our leaders are manipulated by the Republican Party, or by Big Business, or by any one of a thousand different entities.

Here is the inconvenient truth: in February 2009 we had zero dollars and less than seven days to take on a government that had vast amounts of power it had demonstrated it was unafraid to use to quash dissent. A government led by a man all but anointed king by his followers, who had unlimited access to the mainstream media, and whom, we were told, it would be "racist" to criticize.

In retrospect, the allegations leveled against the Tea Party are laughable. Not only did we not have the time, the money, or the connections to "manufacture" a national movement; doing so would have gone directly against our core beliefs as patriotic, Constitution-loving Americans. Our opponents' failure to understand the true nature of our movement says more about them than us.

So what were our original goals as stated on that conference call that took place on February 20, 2009? They were fairly modest. We hoped to organize a few small gatherings across the country, perhaps five or ten, with a few hundred attendees at most, to tell our government that we were not going to take it anymore. We had no call centers or direct-mail operations or phalanxes of union activists or chartered buses. All we had was Facebook and Twitter and the courage of our convictions.

Seven days later, on February 27, 2009, in the middle of a brutally cold winter, forty-nine tea party protests were held all across America. What started a week before with a conference call had blossomed into a movement that was thirty-five thousand Tea Partiers strong and growing.

Five days later, in early March 2009, we formalized our group and gave it a name: Tea Party Patriots. By *formalized* we mean: we registered teapartypatriots.org and called in some personal favors to put up a makeshift Web site and Facebook page. We didn't even have a logo. What we did have was a date for our next tea party rallies. April 15, 2009. Tax Day.

While "Astroturf" organizations spend big money to drive traffic to their Web sites, our Web site—which had no money, no advertising, and minimal functionality—was quickly deluged with traffic. It crashed repeatedly as amateur, first-time tea party activists sent us their events to post online, and people who were searching for tea party events somehow wound up on our page. Forty-eight hours before the Tax Day tea parties, we were so overwhelmed with requests that we had no choice but to simply give up posting new events.

On April 15, 2009, the date that most Tea Partiers will tell you is when the movement truly began, more than 1.2 million people attended more than 850 tea party events across the country.

We were not alone after all.

∼

So how did we grow from twenty-two people to 1.2 million people in less than two months?

We did not fully realize it at the time, but we were organizing the Tea Party movement along the lines of an *open-source* community. In the world of computer software, open-source communities develop and improve ideas organically, based on concepts and practices that work. Driven by innovation contributed by individuals, *open source* simply means that a system is available to any who wish to contribute. It provides the fastest possible rate of improvement for ideas, and in the case of the Tea Party movement, this notion was fundamental to the development of a true political revolution. In the software world an individual—or a small core of individuals—creates a spark or *source code*, then introduces it to a larger audience. If the idea is deemed useful, others begin to copy and expand the code base. In the Tea Party movement, the original source code, developed on the February 20 conference call, looked something like this:

> A tea party is a public protest against big, invasive government, organized through online means, but intended to take place in the offline world.

After the real-world events were held, the organizers returned to the online world to share their experiences. Communicating through Facebook, Twitter, e-mail, and conference calls, they shared their excitement and the lessons they had learned. Through this open-source feedback loop, the core of the Tea Party movement matured.

In Sacramento, California, organizers learned that if they wanted to hold a protest on the grounds of the state capitol, they needed a permit.

In Atlanta, Georgia, organizers learned that if you're going to hold a rally for five hundred people, you have to have a stage and a PA system, and contributed this knowledge.

The Tea Party movement is now populated with online educational tools, press releases, software, music, art, and advice on how to run a nonprofit. All of it developed in a true open-source fashion. This is more than an "angry mob." This is a new political paradigm. It allows for the development of tools, technology, education, activism, and ultimately political influence at a rate not available to previous movements. With millions of contributors actively participating in a national community that is growing daily, the Tea Party Patriots, and the Tea Party movement at large, have changed the political landscape forever.

The alternative to open-source development is what is known as a *closed system*. The Republican and Democratic parties both work this way. In closed systems, ideas originate only at the top of the pyramid. They are then handed down through layers of bureaucracy, and the people charged with implementing those ideas are given little input and even less latitude. Because of the hierarchical nature of these systems, they are slow to change, almost impervious to new ideas, and slow to grow. Rather than encouraging innovation, they lock in the status quo, discourage dissent, kill novelty, and reward those who hoard information, instead of sharing it with everyone. Sounds like a pretty good description of our government, too, doesn't it?

~

After the initial round of tea parties, our movement found itself at a crossroads. We had become good at articulating what we were against. But to be a viable force in American politics, we had to work together to figure out what the movement was going to stand for, what our goals were, and how we would achieve those goals. Thankfully, the open-source movement allowed for the spontaneous creation of order from what seemed like chaos.

Guided by a Tea Party Patriot from Ohio, Scott Boston, the activists voluntarily worked together to articulate the core values of our movement. First, we developed a simple rule to determine whether an idea would be incorporated into our philosophy or rejected. When an idea was raised, we would vote on it. If more than 60 percent of the grassroots coordinators agreed, we would consider it ours.

Over a period of several months, we engaged in online debate and discussion over what the core values and the mission statement of the Tea Party Patriots would be. Ultimately, we arrived at the following mission statement:

> The impetus for the Tea Party movement is excessive government spending and taxation. Our mission is to attract, educate, organize, and mobilize our fellow citizens to secure public policy consistent with our three core values of Fiscal Responsibility, Constitutionally Limited Government and Free Markets.

And we decided on how to best articulate each of those core values like this:

Fiscal Responsibility. Fiscal responsibility by government honors and respects the freedom of the individual to spend the money that is the fruit of their own labor. A constitutionally limited government, designed to protect the blessings of liberty, must be fiscally responsible or it must subject its citizenry to high levels of taxation that unjustly restrict the liberty our Constitution was designed to protect. Such runaway deficit spending as we now see in Washington, D.C., compels us to take action as the increasing national debt is a grave threat to our national sovereignty and the personal and economic liberty of future generations.

Constitutionally Limited Government. We, the members of the Tea Party Patriots, are inspired by our founding documents and regard the Constitution of the United States to be the supreme law of the land. We believe that it is possible to know the original intent of the government our Founders set forth, and stand in support of that intent. Like the Founders, we support states' rights for those powers not expressly stated in the Constitution. As the government is of the people, by the people and for the people, in all other matters we support the personal liberty of the individual, within the rule of law.

Free Markets. A free market is the economic consequence of personal liberty. The Founders believed that personal and economic freedom were indivisible, as do we. Our current government's interference distorts the free market and inhibits the pursuit of individual and economic liberty. Therefore, we support a return to the free-market principles on which this nation was founded and oppose government intervention into the operations of private business.

We went on to articulate our philosophy this way:

Tea Party Patriots, Inc., as an organization, believes in Fiscal Responsibility, Constitutionally Limited Government, and Free Markets. Tea Party Patriots, Inc. is a non-partisan grassroots organization of individuals united by our core values, which derive from the Declaration of Independence, the Constitution of the United States of America, and the Bill of Rights as explained in *The Federalist Papers*. We recognize and support the strength of a grassroots organization powered by activism and civic responsibility at a local level.

We hold that the United States is a republic conceived by its architects as a nation whose people were granted "unalienable rights" by our Creator. Chief among these are the rights to "life, liberty and the pursuit of happiness." The Tea Party Patriots stand with our Founders, as heirs to the Republic, to claim our rights and duties which preserve their legacy and our own. We hold, as did the Founders, that there exists an inherent benefit to our country when private property and prosperity are secured by natural law and the rights of the individual.

As an organization we do not take stances on social issues. We urge members to engage fully on the social issues they consider important and aligned with their beliefs.

Issues like abortion and gay marriage have little to do with our three core principles, and therefore we leave these issues for other groups to advocate.

So why has Tea Party Patriots grown so big so quickly, without any prodding, direction, or central control? What is it about the Tea Party movement that resonated so profoundly with so many Americans? Here is the answer that our detractors and attackers and opponents are terrified to admit but, deep down, know is true. The reason for the success of the modern-day Tea Party movement is that our "source code" is the same as America's. Our founding principles are the same as America's. These beliefs are in Americans' DNA; they are each American's birthright. And this source code is favored by an overwhelming majority of American citizens.

Those who oppose fiscal responsibility, constitutionally limited government, and free markets are free to argue against these principles.

But those who do—whether Republicans or Democrats, liberal or conservative—will soon find themselves in a permanent minority and on the losing side of history.

We saw this dynamic play out in stark relief in the 2010 midterm elections. Candidates who supported our three core values were overwhelmingly elected. Those who did not were defeated, either in the primaries or in the general election.

After our massive victories in 2010, we had three choices. We could collapse under our own weight and allow the movement to be co-opted by special interests (most likely the Republican Party); we could declare victory and go home (though our members were beginning to realize that eternal vigilance truly *is* the price of liberty); or we could press on to begin planning for America's future.

We chose the future.

~

The first step in restoring America's founding principles is for all of us to realize that our nation's decline did not happen overnight. Rather, it has taken us a hundred years or more to reach our present state of crisis. In each decade, our liberty has slipped away a little more. It took the vast acceleration of this phenomenon over the past ten years to awaken the sleeping giant of America. Those of us who are now in the majority are ready to get America back on track. We have strength in numbers, we have faith in our principles, and we are ready to fight and win.

What we lost over a century we cannot win back overnight. For too long, career politicians, motivated primarily by the desire to increase their own power, and supported by the beneficiaries of their largesse, have adopted a short-term approach to government. Thinking in two-, four-, or six-year cycles, they have ignored the long-term consequences of their actions, while they line their own pockets and the pockets of their cronies, and erode our freedoms.

Using the open-source model, we developed a Forty-Year Plan to restore America's founding principles, and to restore America's greatness. We call this plan the Tea Party Patriots' Forty-Year Plan and it contains Five Pathways to Liberty.

In this book, we examine what has happened to America in five critical areas: economics, politics, education, the judiciary, and culture. We look at how deviating from the principles of the Founding Fathers led to the decline of America, and then propose five specific Pathways to Liberty to help take our country back and restore power to We the People.

The final chapter of this book is a call to arms. And just because it's the last chapter in the book, that doesn't mean it's the last chapter in the movement. It's actually a beginning. The heart of the Tea Party movement is its members and its ability to learn from and be guided by those members. We're constantly learning and growing, incorporating new ideas into our philosophy, and adding members every day. And in the last chapter we'll be telling you how to participate in creating a Forty-Year Plan to save the nation.

We don't claim to know everything about how to run this country. In fact, we don't claim to know *anything* about how to run this country. But we know what kind of country we want our children and our grandchildren to live in. And more important, we know *who* should be running the country: patriots, just like you.

So we invite you to take the concepts we put forth here and make them better. If you have an idea about how to improve our country, we don't just want to hear it, we *need* to hear it. The open-source nature of the Tea Party movement means that we can incorporate great ideas more quickly than any other movement in history. And we've set up a section of our Web site specifically to listen to you. After you read this book, go to http://www.teapartypatriots.org/40yearplan to contribute. Not only will the best ideas submitted and judged by patriots be included in the next edition of this book, but we'll activate our whole movement to make them a reality.

This is your opportunity to change the world, and it starts with saving the United States of America. The journey to take back our country starts here and now.

★ 2 ★

What the Tea Party Believes about Economics

It is the duty of the patriot to protect his country from his government.

—THOMAS PAINE

I place economy among the first and most important virtues, and public debt as the greatest of dangers to be feared . . . To preserve our independence, we must not let our rulers load us with perpetual debt . . . We must make our choice between economy and liberty or profusion and servitude.

—THOMAS JEFFERSON

HOW MUCH IS a trillion dollars?

Few of us will ever even see a million dollars all at once in our lifetimes. Even fewer of us will see a billion. And no human being, in the history of the world, has ever amassed a trillion dollars.

That is why, for most of us, a million dollars or a billion dollars are abstract concepts. And a trillion dollars is an abstract concept for everyone, except the U.S. government.

If we could point to one thing that sparked the Tea Party movement, it was our shared dismay over our government's overspending, which put America trillions of dollars into debt.

To the ear, a *trillion* sounds a lot like a *million* or a *billion*. The words even rhyme. To the eye, only two or three letters separate them as words. Represented numerically, most of us are lost after six zeroes other than knowing that such numbers represent offensively large amounts of government spending.

Politicians intuitively understand that we have a hard time getting our heads around the concept of a *trillion*. They also understand that the barrier to a trillion dollars is largely emotional; it is not grounded in the personal experiences of the average American citizen. Still, emotions are powerful drivers in politics. That is why the Bush and Obama administrations worked hard to keep their stimulus packages and spending packages below that emotional barrier. George W. Bush's Stimulus 1 was proposed at around $700 billion (but wound up being more). The Obama administration did everything it could (even removing doctors' payments and fudging numbers) to ensure the price tag for "Obamacare" came in under a trillion dollars. But, at some point along the line, the one-trillion-dollar emotional barrier was breached, which opened an even bigger floodgate for big-government spenders to spend your current—and future—taxpayer dollars.

Right now, the U.S. government is budgeting to spend roughly $1 trillion more than it will take in for fiscal year 2012. It's a rough estimate because Congress and the administration constantly manipulate the numbers and each new proposal changes the bottom line. One thing remains certain: all of them intend to spend far more than the government brings in. And they intend to do it for many years to come.

That's $1 trillion in *new* government overspending, on top of Stimulus 1, after Stimulus 2, and after the government bailed out hundreds of banks, General Motors, Chrysler, AIG, Fannie Mae and Freddie Mac (and, through them, more than two-thirds of U.S. mortgages), after the Federal Reserve's "Quantitative Easing 1," after "Quantitative Easing 2," after the government took over the student loan industry, and after it rammed through Obamacare against the will of the people; this massive government power-grab, if not repealed, will cost more than one trillion dollars and turn control of more than one-sixth of the entire U.S. economy over to Washington.

After all that spending, and after the American people whacked

Congress with the biggest midterm shellacking of any U.S. government in three generations, the federal government went ahead and budgeted to overspend an *additional* trillion dollars above its projected revenues. As reported in *Forbes*, "Simple math says that a $1.1 trillion deficit on a $3.8 trillion budget is 'overspending' by 40%."

When a government *budgets* to overspend its revenues by a trillion dollars, it means that it is *planning* to overspend its revenues by a trillion dollars. If we give the government more credit than it has shown it deserves by trusting that it will not exceed even that insanely large amount, the U.S. government will spend, in less than twelve months, a trillion dollars above and beyond all the money it already plans to take from us. Which means, after we have paid all of our taxes, and after each American household is plunged $30,000 deeper into debt by this government's *current* level of overspending, we will be on the hook for an *additional* trillion dollars. This year.

So, how much *is* a trillion dollars?

Since all of this government overspending is money that you will owe, let us look at it in terms of how much *time* it will take for you to pay it back.

- To pay back one *million* dollars, at the rate of one dollar per second, would take you eleven and a half days.
- To pay back one *billion* dollars, at the rate of one dollar per second, would take you thirty-two *years*.
- To pay back one *trillion* dollars, at the rate of one dollar per second, would take you *thirty-two thousand years*.

But wait.

You probably don't earn anything close to one dollar per second. The median American *household* income is about $50,000 per year. That translates to less than one-tenth of one cent per second. So if your family earns $50,000 per year, and if you spend none of that on food, rent, transportation, income tax, or even pursuing your own happiness, and if you take all of your family's household income and use it, not to pay down the government's *current* debt, but just to pay down the one trillion dollars in *new* debt that the government is *planning* to overspend *this* year—it would take your family *32 million years* to pay for it.

Ready to join an "angry mob" yet?

If you are not angry, you are not paying attention. The good news is that if you are reading this book, you *are*. You have also probably been angry at some point over the past years, as you watched the government spend all of the money you will ever make in your lifetime and all of the money your children will ever make in their lifetimes.

Government overspending is not an abstract problem. It is the central problem of our time. When America was hit on 9/11, it was an act of war. When America is hit by hurricanes or floods or wildfires, those are acts of nature. But when America gets hit by a tidal wave of spending, it is an act of cowardice—or worse—by our elected representatives. Thomas Jefferson, principal author of the Declaration of Independence, called this kind of deficit spending "the greatest of dangers to be feared," and he said that "to preserve our independence, we must not let our rulers load us with perpetual debt."

Government overspending is a self-inflicted problem. Which means we can put an end to this problem by holding our representatives' feet to the fire, getting them to honor the oaths they swore to uphold, and stopping them from inflicting generational harm to America by spending trillions of dollars we simply do not have.

As James Madison wrote in Federalist 51, "If angels were to govern men, neither external nor internal controls on government would be necessary." Since America is hardly governed by angels, the Tea Party Patriots are critically important to America's future. Our (unfortunately necessary) role is to act as a persistent, external control on government. We know we'll never get perfect people to represent us; they don't exist. Even the politicians who claim to be on our side—and who would not hold the positions of power they hold today without the power of our votes—tend to drift into big government spending the moment they are not being watched. That is why the Tea Party Patriots have to swat the Republican leadership, often several times a week, to stop them from driving America into insolvency at only a slightly slower speed than the Democrats.

One party [the Democrats] wants to floor it and put its foot on the pedal as we go over the cliff, and another party [the Republicans] says oh, no, no, no, it's okay, vote for us, we're only going to go over the cliff in third gear.

—MARK STEYN,
on the *Hugh Hewitt Show*, March 17, 2011

When government spends your money against your will, it destroys your liberty to use your money however you see fit. A dollar is a unit of power. When you keep that dollar, you are keeping a unit of power that you earned. When you spend that dollar, you are exercising your right to spend your own money (power) according to your own will (liberty). When the government spends your money against your will, it is taking away your power and your liberty to direct your power to pursue your own happiness.

America was founded on the Declaration of Independence, which states that your liberty, and your pursuit of happiness, are "unalienable rights." For the first time in history, a nation—America—was built upon the notion that your rights do not come from kings or governments, but directly from the Creator to you. It is the job of all American governments to secure your rights, not to grant them or take them away. The Declaration of Independence also recognized that governments derive "their just powers from the consent of the governed." Did we, the governed, consent to have this or any government take away our God-given rights, and the God-given rights of our children and grandchildren, to liberty and the pursuit of happiness? No. That is why the Declaration also said that "whenever any Form of Government becomes destructive of these ends, it is the Right of the People to alter or to abolish it, and to institute new Government."

These are not just a handful of words in some dusty old history book. They are the revolutionary words that built this nation and set America above and beyond all other nations. Every great society in world history has had a head start of hundreds, and sometimes thousands, of years on America. And yet in just over two hundred years, America surpassed them all to become the greatest, most powerful, most successful nation in world history. The jury is in. The American experiment worked. Our founding principles are the right founding principles, as evidenced by the fact that America is, at the time of this writing, the most powerful and prosperous nation in the history of the world.

When our Founding Fathers declared their independence in 1776, only thirty months had passed since the first American tea party on December 16, 1773. What provoked our forefathers to rise up and dump British tea into Boston Harbor? Tax. They were not angry about the rising price of tea. The price of tea actually went down back in 1773, when the British lowered its cost in order to coerce the American settlers into agreeing with the concept of their tea being taxed by the Crown. So the cost of tea actually went down, and yet our forefathers *still* rose up in the first American tea party (and provoked a long and bloody war against a far more powerful British adversary) on principle alone: the principle that a distant, foreign government should not have the right to arbitrarily tax us.

> *Europe was created by history. America was created by philosophy.*
>
> —Margaret Thatcher

That was how the first American Revolution began. That was how our nation began. On principle. The principle that our liberty, and our right to pursue our happiness, are God-given rights that are not to be infringed upon by government.

What did it take for the second American Revolution, the modern-day American Tea Party movement, to begin?

By now, you have heard all the false and slanderous descriptions of us Tea Partiers. So here is a more truthful way to describe us: patient. We are far more tolerant and patient than our forefathers, who rose up and sparked a revolution against a government which, though tyrannical, was much less involved in our daily lives.

When our government introduced an income tax in 1862 as a temporary wartime measure, we did not rise up. When it made that "temporary" tax measure permanent in 1913, we did not rise up. When our tax burden rose from 2 to 3 to 5 percent, 10 percent, 20 percent, and all the way up to 40–50 percent for individuals today, we remained silent. We did not stage a revolution when the government taxed our coffee, our sodas, our cigarettes, or our beer. We did not revolt when it taxed food that tastes good, or the cars we drive in to get that food, or the gas we use to power our cars, or the plastic bags we use to carry our food home. We did not rise up when it created vast, expensive, and unaccountable bureaucracies to seize control over our commerce, our workplaces, transportation, energy, treasury, charity, justice, the ground we walk upon, the air we breathe, the water we drink, the food we eat, our security, the arts, and the education of our children.

Only after the government seized control over our banks, our mortgages, our cars, our insurance, *and* took dead aim at controlling our health—*our very lives*—along with one-sixth of the entire U.S. economy, while going into debt for more money than all of us produce in an entire year—only *then* did we rise up in the second American Revolution: the modern-day Tea Party movement.

∽

There is a reason why Thomas Jefferson placed "economy among the first and most important virtues." The right economics led to America's greatness. The wrong economics could lead to America's downfall.

When we Tea Party Patriots call for "economic reform," we are not calling for economic revolution. We are calling for a return to the basics. Basics that *work*, as evidenced by the fact that America has had the number one economy in the history of the world. Basics that, when ignored or forgotten or thwarted, diminish America's economic standing in the world, as evidenced by the fact that the American economy is now slipping, and slipping fast, against many of the world's other economies.

Before we get into the Tea Party Patriots' specific plans for economic reform, it is critically important that we clearly understand some basic economic principles—principles that are self-evident to the American people, but not to our elected representatives.

To begin with, where does wealth come from? Our elected representatives may believe that it comes from a printing press. But that's only money; it's not wealth. True wealth comes about in just one of two ways. The first is through human labor and ingenuity. When we plow a field and plant seeds, we take something that is virtually worthless and turn it into something that can sustain human life. When we take steel and rubber and transform them into a car through hard work and intelligence, we create a whole that is greater than the sum of its parts. Likewise, when a pharmaceutical company creates a drug, or an author writes a book, or a baker combines flour, yeast, and water to make bread, wealth—value—is created.

The other way wealth is generated is by making sure that resources are efficiently allocated. The very act of getting something into the hands of someone who values it the most creates wealth. A gallon of gasoline is worth more to a person who owns a car than to one who doesn't. The mechanism that ensures that things achieve their highest value is free-market capitalism. Every time a transaction takes place in a free market, wealth is created.

Consider a hungry woman who meets a thirsty woman. The hungry woman can have all the water in the world, but to her it is less valuable than one morsel of food. Likewise, to the thirsty woman, all the food in the world pales in comparison to a glass of water. When we voluntarily exchange something we have too much of for something we don't have enough of, both parties wind up better off than when they started.

This principle becomes slightly more complicated when you introduce currency into the equation, but the result is the same. If you offer me a dollar for my banana, there will be one of two outcomes. Either I will accept your deal, because that dollar (and the things I can buy with it) is worth more to me than the banana, or I will reject it, because the banana is worth more to me than that dollar. Similarly, if the dollar was worth more to *you* than the banana, you wouldn't offer me that dollar for it in the first place.

However, when the government spends a dollar, that same mechanism doesn't operate, because there's no way for the government to know what's most valuable to you. It takes your money and spends it on things that benefit its favored constituencies. Perhaps your dollar was, in fact, worth more to you than my banana. If the government taxes you in order to support banana farmers, you're *worse* off than you would be under the free-market system—even if the government gives you a banana. In practice, of course, for the tax dollars we contribute, we're much more likely to get . . . peanuts.

How widespread is this phenomenon? The appendix to the 2012 U.S. government budget—not the whole budget, just the appendix—is 1,364 pages long. Since we brought up the subject of peanuts, buried in this appendix is a government proposal to spend $94,755,000 of your tax dollars on a government program that provides marketing services for the producers of seventeen specific agricultural products, including cotton, honey, watermelons, popcorn, lamb, mangoes, and, of course, peanuts.

What if you're a cranberry farmer? Can funds from this program be spent on cranberry marketing? Fortunately, not. But they can be spent on marketing avocados.

Angry yet?

Buried deeper in that appendix, on page 888, is the listing of a government program called the National Infrastructure Bank, which is a brand-new bureaucracy with a mandate to spend billions of your hard-earned dollars on . . . something. Infrastructure. What kind of infrastructure is unclear from the appendix. But either way, right beneath the budget header for "National Infrastructure Bank," and before the budget itemizes the billions of your dollars it plans to spend, you should notice the words *not subject to PAYGO.*

What is this *PAYGO* that the National Infrastructure Bank is not subject to? It is the concept that governments should "pay-as-they-go," meaning they should only pay for programs with money that they have already taken from you (taxpayer dollars), not money that they will have to take from you and your children and your grandchildren in the future (debt). *PAYGO* is a new concept for the American government, but it is not a new concept for the American people. You, and most responsible Americans, already know that you cannot spend money that you do not have. You also know that if you absolutely must spend money that you do not have (on big-ticket items like cars or your family home), you must borrow that money, which means going into debt—debt that you must then pay back.

This is a revolutionary concept for governments. And so, when they do stumble upon what we the people call "common sense," they praise themselves and wrap it in new, flashy names like PAYGO. Here is what then-Speaker of the House Nancy Pelosi said when Congress passed a new PAYGO law back in February of 2010: "When I became Speaker of the House . . . our majority made PAYGO the rule of the House—that if you wanted to have an investment, an entitlement, etc., you had to pay for it. There was no open-ended spending."

Did our government follow its own law?

Not according to the budget scholar Brian Riedl, who observed that "Congress waived PAYGO every time it proved even slightly inconvenient." Congress waived it for the $787 billion "stimulus" bill. And waived it on page 888 of the 2012 budget for the National Infrastructure Bank, which is "not subject to PAYGO."

How much was earmarked for this new, big-government bureaucracy? It is $5 billion for one fiscal year (including $70 million to administer this $5 billion). Oh, and that $5 billion is "to remain available until expended." Which means, if those 70 million dollars' worth of administrators spend your money as fast as they can and if, at the end of the year, they find themselves with "more money left that year," they get to keep all of your money that they didn't have time to spend, instead of giving it back to you.

If there are not enough hours in the year for 70 million dollars' worth of administrators to spend your money, perhaps they are trying to spend too much of it. Of course, governments do not think this way. According to the way governments think, if they fail to spend all of your money on schedule, your money will "remain available until expended." Then, next year, they will probably hire more administrators to give your money away more quickly, because clearly 70 million dollars' worth of administrators cannot shovel your money out the door fast enough.

It is no accident that of the three core principles of the Tea Party Patriots, two of them—fiscal responsibility and free markets—are economic principles. Let us look at each of these fundamental economic principles individually.

FISCAL RESPONSIBILITY

What is fiscal responsibility?

Each time you make the choice to not spend more money than you have, you demonstrate fiscal responsibility. If you have ten dollars in your pocket, it would be fiscally responsible to spend less than ten dollars, perhaps prudent to save some of that ten dollars for the future, but it would be fiscally irresponsible for you to spend all of the money in your pocket.

When a government reaches into someone else's pocket and spends all of their money, it is beyond fiscally irresponsible. Because it is not the government's money. And it is profoundly disrespectful to spend all of someone else's money on something that they would have never spent it on themselves, like a bloated government bureaucracy. It is a despotic insult to We the People to spend all of our money, when we clearly said at the ballot box that we want our government to spend less. And it is grounds for revolution when a government spends all of the money the people will *ever* earn, for generations to come, against the will of the people.

> *I am for a government rigorously frugal & simple, applying all the possible savings of the public revenue to the discharge of the national debt; and not for a multiplication of officers & salaries merely to make parti-*

sans, & for increasing, by every device, the public debt,
on the principle of its being a public blessing.

—THOMAS JEFFERSON,
letter to Elbridge Gerry, January 26, 1799

Politicians always wrap their fiscal irresponsibility in the cloak of "a public blessing." When they seized hundreds of American banks, backstopped trillions in bad mortgages, propped up two of America's three car companies, took control over the world's biggest insurer, and nationalized one-sixth of the American economy through Obamacare—they sold all of this fiscal irresponsibility as "a public blessing."

Some Americans, and most of the American media, bought into this explanation. They are now beginning to realize that they were sold a bag of big-spending lies. Those of us in the Tea Party movement never bought the government's lies, because we know that it is not the role of an American government to seize private assets from the people, or to remove risk from a risk-based capitalist system, no

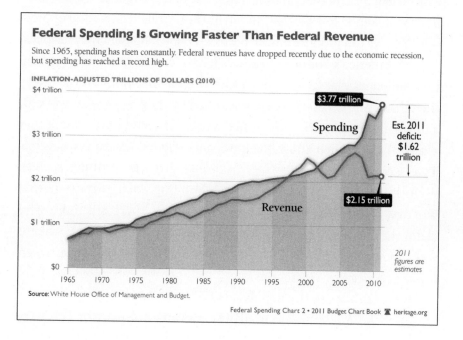

Federal Spending Is Growing Faster Than Federal Revenue

Since 1965, spending has risen constantly. Federal revenues have dropped recently due to the economic recession, but spending has reached a record high.

INFLATION-ADJUSTED TRILLIONS OF DOLLARS (2010)

$3.77 trillion

Spending

Est. 2011 deficit: $1.62 trillion

Revenue

$2.15 trillion

2011 figures are estimates

Source: White House Office of Management and Budget.

Federal Spending Chart 2 • 2011 Budget Chart Book ☎ heritage.org matter what kind of "public blessing" the government labels it. Even if the U.S. government had seized all of that money and liberty and trashed the philosophical foundations of capitalism—while balancing the books—it would have still been wrong on principle. But, as we all now know, it was also wrong in practice. It did not work. America is still in the midst of a long and profound economic slowdown, while the projected level of government spending for fiscal year 2010 is almost double the amount of government spending just ten years ago, and 75 percent above projected government revenues. (The White House projections, February 2011. See the chart on page 37.)

In other words: fiscally irresponsible government spending did not, and does not, help the economy. In the words of Thomas Jefferson, "The principle of spending money to be paid by posterity [is] swindling futurity on a large scale."

Another word for spent money to be paid by posterity is *debt*. In the words of George Washington, "There is no practice more dangerous than that of borrowing money" and "To contract new debts is not the way to pay old ones." Thomas Jefferson later expanded on our first president's words: "A departure from principle in one instance becomes a precedent for [another] and the forehorse of this frightful team is public debt. Taxation follows that, and in its train wretchedness and oppression. Yes, we did produce a near-perfect republic. But will they keep it?"

Did America's Founding Fathers have a crystal ball that could see the challenges that face America today? Of course not. But they were thoughtful and learned men who studied the history of what worked, and what did not work, and crafted a new system of government that placed the governed above the governors and held fiscal responsibility as a core principle.

Although the Tea Party Patriots' founding documents state that our first core principle is fiscal responsibility, there are those who claim the Tea Party movement ignored fiscal irresponsibility when it was practiced by Republicans, and was only roused to action when it was practiced by Democrats.

Not true. Just ask the Republicans.

True, the modern-day Tea Party movement began in February

2009, when the White House, the Senate, and the House of Representatives were all controlled by Democrats. But the first stirrings of our movement started with the out-of-control spending of the Republican George W. Bush administration—which gathered steam in his second term and came to a head with President Bush's big government bailouts in September of 2008.

But as we said before, and as our actions have shown, we are patient revolutionaries. It was only after a Republican government, and then a Democratic government, seized so much of our economy and drove America so dangerously deep into debt with its overspending that our quiet revolution made its voice heard.

The transformation that the Tea Party movement sparked in our national debate is profound. For the first time in a generation—and perhaps for the first time ever—We the People are demanding that our government do *less*. To stop "bringing home the bacon." To stop spending us into debt under the guise of it being "a public blessing."

It is impossible to overstate the magnitude of this shift. What the American people are saying, through the Tea Party movement, is: "Government, stop giving us 'free' money." Because we understand that the amount of money being spent right now by the U.S. government is so large that no living American will be alive when those bills come due, or when those bills come close to getting paid. Yes, there may be some present-day consequences like a sluggish economy and a struggling job market. But these consequences pale in comparison to the historical consequences that future generations will face, in a world in which America may no longer be the world's number one power.

> *Remember, democracy never lasts long. It soon wastes, exhausts, and murders itself. There was never a democracy that did not commit suicide.*
>
> —JOHN ADAMS

The modern-day Tea Party movement was slow to boil. But it's taking action now, lest the greatest nation in the history of the world waste, exhaust, and destroy itself through a lack of fiscal responsibility.

FREE MARKETS

Why are free markets important? Why are they worth fighting for? What makes a free-market system better than other systems?

In addition to being one of the only ways to actually create wealth, the free market gives people (and companies and countries) the freedom to fail. The freedom to fail is a necessary component of a free market. When a government declares—as both the Bush Republicans and Obama Democrats did—that certain players in our economy are "too big to fail," it undercuts the very foundation of America's free-market economy. When responsibilities of failure are removed from a free-market economic system, the consequences for bad behavior are also removed. If there are no consequences for bad economic behavior, bad economic behavior will continue and even grow. Removing the risk of failure also removes the rewards of adhering to America's founding free-market principles and bestows rewards upon those who have become expert at gaming this new system of insider favors and backroom deals.

To paraphrase the economist Walter E. Williams: once a free-market system is gamed to embrace a system of payoffs and backroom deals, it is no longer in the self-interest of people to play by free-market rules. Which makes the actions of Tea Partiers even more remarkable. If self-interest were our only motivator, it would make more sense for us to jump into the government cesspool and try to get our share of the government's largesse.

And yet millions of Americans, from every state in the nation, are rising up to demand that their government give them back the freedom to fail. Think about that.

Thomas West, professor of politics at the University of Dallas and a senior fellow at the Claremont Institute, captured the zeitgeist of today's media, experts, and government when he wrote, "Many economists claim that the modern economy is subject to 'market failure,' or the inability of free markets to provide a fair allocation of goods and services. This view assumes that current knowledge of economics and production is unquestionably superior to that of the long-dead amateurs who founded the American regime."

These "amateurs" indisputably crafted the most successful-in-practice free-market capitalist system in world history. As evidenced by the fact that, in the historical blink of an eye, America leapfrogged every "enlightened" system in the history of the world to become the greatest economic power the world has ever seen.

We have all heard the old refrain that communism and socialism are great in theory, just not in practice. But the fact that they repeatedly fail in practice, as they are failing again today in America, is evidence that they are wrong in theory. The fact that America's free-market system *worked* in practice is evidence that it was right in theory.

Further evidence that America's free-market system works in both theory and practice can be found in the increasing degree to which America fails as it moves farther away from its free-market principles.

Still, we are told by our politicians and so-called experts that the Founders' view of economics is obsolete and cannot address the problems of today's complex industrial society. They are wrong. The current more "enlightened" view of economics is what is driving the American economy off a cliff. As John Adams said, "Facts are stubborn things."

The facts are on our side. Emotion is on the side of our opponents. They repeatedly use emotionally charged stories of victims (often children and seniors) to scare the public into accepting their theories. But if their concepts ever worked in practice, they would never have to scare anyone into accepting them. They used horror stories of financial market collapse to seize control over the basic plumbing of financial markets. They used frightening anecdotes of families losing their homes to seize control of the majority of all U.S. single-family home loans. And they evoked people's fear of dying to make way for a federal takeover of the U.S. health-care system and to turn the management of our health, our very lives, into public utilities, essentially creatures of Congress and the Health and Human Services Department.

Instead of free-market capitalism, over the past hundred years we have steadily adopted a system in which individuals and companies are allowed to keep private profits, but in which all of us must pay for their losses. Such a system encourages irrational risk-taking and was a direct cause of the recent financial meltdown. Quite simply, our markets are no longer free.

- If our financial markets were free, those who behave badly would be punished (instead of being bailed out by the government) and the system would be open, not closed as it is now to all but a handful of cronies and insiders.
- If our housing market were a free market, your neighbors would not have been given government-subsidized mortgages they could not afford. The only people who would have been harmed by defaults on those mortgages would be the shareholders of the financial institutions who made them.
- And if our health-care system, which still operates somewhat on free-market principles, were to be run by the same people who gave us the post office and the DMV, we would find ourselves waiting (and dying) in the same long lines that are the hallmark of every non-free–market health-care system in the world.

That is why the Tea Party Patriots—and some of the greatest patriots in America's history—support and embrace free markets.

> We who live in free market societies believe that growth,
> prosperity and ultimately human fulfillment, are cre-
> ated from the bottom up, not the government down.
> Only when the human spirit is allowed to invent and
> create, only when individuals are given a personal
> stake in deciding economic policies and benefitting

from their success—only then can societies remain eco-
nomically alive, dynamic, progressive, and free.

—RONALD REAGAN

In the next chapter, you'll see some examples of what must be done to restore fiscal responsibility and free markets to our country, and how we can return the benefits of capitalism to America and get our country back on the right track.

★ 3 ★

The Economic Pathway to Liberty

If industry and labor are left to take their own course, they will generally be directed to those objects which are the most productive, and this in a more certain and direct manner than the wisdom of the most enlightened legislature could point out.

—James Madison

AS WE LOOK ahead and plan for the next forty years, we must never lose sight of the fact that America is a nation that was built on fundamentally correct principles. These principles have been proven to work in practice, and when they're ignored, failure is the result.

Glenn C. Graber's *cut-flower thesis* of morality states that morality cannot endure when it is cut from its roots. So too will America's prosperity wither when cut from the roots that nourish it. Not immediately, of course. As we all know, flowers look vibrant after they have been cut. But eventually, without the nourishment that comes through its roots, every cut flower will die.

In America today, the foundational roots of our economic prosperity are being cut by the very people who swore oaths to nurture and protect them.

Politicians think short term, like someone picking a flower to enjoy for the moment. We must think long term, like farmers who plan beyond the next harvest. For the long run, the only way to ensure economic growth is to study and guard the principles that have graced America with the greatest prosperity in world history. We must guard against those who work to destroy our economic roots, either intentionally or through well-intentioned ineptitude.

In the previous chapter we discussed the imminent economic challenges facing our nation. We saw that the greatest threats to our way of life come from our fellow Americans, from those who are elected to represent us.

Despite proclamations from politicians and the media on the left that America is in recovery and we can all relax, we in the Tea Party movement know the truth. The Great Recession is upon us. Things are bad, and they are not getting better. In fact, it appears they are getting worse.

What is holding America back? Why is its economy suffering? Why are so many people still unemployed? As of August 2011, the Bureau of Labor Statistics reported a 9.1 percent unemployment rate. That statistic does not include the underemployed and the hundreds of thousands of people who have simply lost hope and given up looking. In reality, almost one in five Americans who would like to work simply cannot find a good job. With unemployment historically averaging less than 6 percent, something is definitely wrong.

The government has pumped billions of dollars of "stimulus" spending into the economy, with President Obama promising that doing so would keep unemployment under 8.5 percent. And yet unemployment is still far higher, inflation is on the rise, food and fuel prices are skyrocketing, and it seems there is no end of trouble ahead for the average American family.

Meanwhile, Washington, D.C., is booming. As of summer 2011, the average sale price for a home in our nation's capital was $415,000. This represented an increase of 7.8 percent, or $30,000, in just three months, and 18.6 percent compared to the prior year. Home prices have appreciated 3.8 percent over the last five years in Washington, D.C., while property values in the rest of the country have plummeted. While the center of government thrives, the rest of the nation is suffering. No surprise there.

So what must we do to return America to the free-market greatness that took us from the Jamestown settlement to the great pioneer migrations to the West, through the industrial revolution, to the moon, and now into the modern era of mobile communications and social media? We have to unlock the spirit of entrepreneurship that has always driven Americans to economic greatness. Men and women invest their time, their smarts, and their money into the economy— not to feed a bloated government or to "spread the wealth around"— because they are motivated by the desire for economic gain. They are motivated by the idea that, through their own hard work and ingenuity, they can improve their lot in life. They are motivated by the American dream. But that dream is now gasping for life in this country, and our government is largely to blame.

> *It is not from the benevolence of the butcher, the brewer,*
> *or the baker that we expect our dinner, but from their*
> *regard to their own interest.*
>
> —ADAM SMITH

We need to get government off our backs and free the people to do what Americans do best: create wealth, jobs, and prosperity.

Historically, the government has been most involved in the American economy in four ways:

- Taxation
- Regulation
- Monetary policy
- Direct spending

Each of these is a lever used by politicians to control and manipulate what was intended by the Founders to operate as a primarily free economy based on private property rights. Yet each of these levers is now intended to replace the wisdom of the market with the wisdom of a "ruling elite" that believes it knows better.

The results speak for themselves. We could take this moment to remind everyone of the repeated and predictable failures of government intervention these past years. But instead, let's ask the following questions. If Stimulus 1 was such a good idea, why did we need a Stimulus 2 or all those other rounds of stimulus under different names? If Quantitative Easing 1 (QE1) was such a good idea, then why QE2—or, even worse, a proposed QE3? If propping up mortgage giants Fannie Mae and Freddie Mac was the right thing to do, why did Fannie Mae report a net loss of $6.5 billion in the first quarter of 2011 and have to come back to the taxpayers for yet another multibillion-dollar bailout? Why are people's homes still being foreclosed upon? Why is the housing market still in collapse? And where are all those jobs we were promised?

The onus is on government to prove the merits of its anticonstitutional, interventionist, never-worked-any-time-they've-ever-been-tried policies. We offer, as a counterpoint, the entire arc of American history, which proves that when we adhere to America's free-market founding principles we succeed. Period. Works *every* time it is tried.

Right now, there are hundreds, if not thousands, of people in Washington, D.C., and in departments of economics at universities around the country who are trying to come up with new programs to help the economy. They truly believe that getting our country back on its feet is a matter of developing a new government program, or figuring out which new infrastructure projects to spend your money on, or which new technologies to subsidize.

The truth is that the American economy is like a muscle car, revving its engines and ready to go, but trapped at a government stoplight. Instead of getting out of the way, and letting the economy roar and speed back to life, the government would rather tax those cars to extinction and waste billions of dollars on high-speed trains that are a drag on the economy, not a driver.

Those who run businesses in America, and who don't depend on huge government subsidies, just want to be left alone. They know where growth comes from. It's not from Washington. The chief economist of the National Federation of Independent Business, William Dunkelberg, put it clearly: small business owners in particular "do not trust the economic policies in place or proposed . . . The U.S. economy faces hurricane force headwinds and the government is at the center of the storm, making an economic recovery very difficult."

Or as Ronald Reagan stated, "Government is not the solution to our problem, government *is* the problem."

So what can we do right now to take the shackles off the American economy? Let's start with our tax system.

TAXATION

The American tax system, both individual and corporate, is incomprehensibly complex and growing worse every day. As a simple measurement of this fact, it is worth noting that the number of pages of federal tax rules increased from an absurd 26,300 in 1984 to an astounding 71,684 in 2011. That's thirty-five times longer than the King James Bible.* And while the average corporate tax rate in the thirty largest industrialized countries has *declined* from 38 to 25.5 percent between 1992 and 2011, our comparable rate is now 39.2 percent.

Canada's corporate tax rate is 16 percent. And its economy is doing better, its unemployment rate is lower, and its dollar is now worth more than ours—none of which was true just three years ago.†

At the individual level, few taxpayers are even capable of figuring out or filing their own income taxes. When America's treasury secretary can't even figure out how to file his own income taxes, as was revealed in January 2009, something is radically wrong.

Individual taxpayers spent an estimated 2.43 billion hours in 2010 complying with America's income tax laws. That is an incredible amount of wasted productivity at the national level. According to the National Taxpayers Union (NTU), "Using the most recently reported average employer cost for civilian workers by the Bureau of Labor Statistics of $29.37 per hour, this time is worth an incredible $71.4 billion!"

And the cost is not just in lost productivity. It's also money directly out of pocket for American taxpayers. Again, according to the NTU, "Individual taxpayers will spend a lot of money too: an estimated

* http://www.cato.org/research/fiscal_policy/facts/tax_charts.html.
† http://www.cato.org/research/fiscal_policy/facts/images/tax-corp.gif.

$31.5 billion this year [2010] for tax software, tax preparers, postage, and other out-of-pocket costs, according to the most recent Internal Revenue Service (IRS) regulatory filing."*

There are serious moral considerations with our tax system as well. Today, more than *half* of American households pay no income tax at all.† That means there are now more *takers* in America than *makers*. Which means the majority of Americans now have a financial incentive to vote themselves more money (government handouts) by supporting wrongheaded government policies that punish the productive.

A family of four, with two children at home, that makes less than $50,000 a year contributes no income taxes to support such things as our national defense, our federal court system—or any other constitutional functions of the federal government. And of those who do pay income taxes, an astonishing number of them now work for the government. As reported in an opinion piece in the *Wall Street Journal*, by Stephen Moore on April 1, 2011, "More Americans work for the government than in manufacturing, farming, fishing, forestry, mining and utilities combined," which is "an almost exact reversal of the situation in 1960." These government employees (takers) have a personal stake in growing the size and scope of government (their employer), and these takers now outnumber America's entire manufacturing industry (makers) by a factor of nearly two to one.

Today, a majority of Americans have no fiscal incentive to oppose income tax increases, because they don't pay them, and an astonishing number of Americans now have a fiscal incentive to grow the size and scope of government, because government is either their employer or their benefactor through government handouts. Such a situation is dangerous and unsustainable, and it must be rectified.

It is time to begin the long fight to restore common sense to the tax codes of the nation, the states, and all the downstream municipalities. It is time to remove the complexity, lower the rates, and reverse a

* http://www.ntu.org/ntu-pp-127-tax-complexity-2010.pdf.
† http://www.finance.senate.gov/newsroom/ranking/download/?id=9fe27e9f-a5e0-4010 -8461-ffc00b5c00ef/.

decades-long trend of crushing individuals and businesses under a tax code that destroys our productivity.

WHAT DO THE TEA PARTY PATRIOTS PROPOSE?

At the national level the most interesting debate is the one between a *flat tax* and a particular kind of national consumption tax called the *fair tax.*

From an economic perspective, there are many similarities between the fair tax and the flat tax. For example:

- Both the fair tax and the flat tax are effectively "consumption taxes." In other words, people are taxed for spending money, not earning it. The flat tax would require citizens to file tax returns the way they do now—although the process would be much less complicated. But under the flat tax, people would only be taxed on the money they spend; that is, the amount they make, minus the amount they save. The fair tax is a retail sales tax that would rely on merchants to collect tax at the point of sale, as they now collect state and local sales taxes.
- Both plans would eliminate the death tax and taxes on capital gains.
- Both plans are single-tax-rate systems that eliminate multiple taxation.
- Both plans would dramatically reduce the time and money Americans spend complying with the current, complicated tax code.

Whether flat tax, fair tax, or some other system, we believe that any such system must tax consumption instead of production. It is a fundamental principle of economics that when you subsidize something you get more of it, and when you tax something, you get less of it. Currently, our national tax system taxes production in the form of income, and not consumption. As a result, we get less production— and less income. That is economic insanity. Punishing production gives us less production and producers. Producers generate jobs, investment capital, wealth, and prosperity. If anything, that is the behavior we should be promoting, not punishing, in our tax code.

REGULATION

I think we have more machinery of government than is necessary, too many parasites living on the labor of the industrious.

—THOMAS JEFFERSON,
letter to William Ludlow, September 6, 1824

It will be of little avail to the people that the laws are made by men of their own choice, if the laws be so voluminous that they cannot be read, or so incoherent that they cannot be understood; if they be repealed or revised before they are promulgated, or undergo such incessant changes that no man who knows what the law is today can guess what it will be tomorrow.

—JAMES MADISON,
Federalist 62, *February 27, 1788*

A 1996 report by the U.S. Joint Economic Committee noted that "regulations work like taxes. It makes no difference to the entrepreneur, or the economy, whether the entrepreneur must write a $5,000 check to the government for taxes or a $5,000 check to comply with a regulation. Forcing the entrepreneur to comply with regulations diverts resources to less-productive uses." In short, regulations waste labor and capital.

Today, entrepreneurs are buried under a pile of regulations based on bills thousands of pages long, passed by a Congress that doesn't bother to read them. And each page can lead to multiple regulations. Need a recent example?

Obamacare, the health-care reform passed against the public will, is a perfect example of government regulation run amok, regulating approximately one-sixth of our economy. And according to *U.S. News and World Report*, the law is a massive regulation multiplier: "Section 3022 of the law, which is about the Medicare shared savings program, takes up just six pages in the 907-page Patient Protection and Affordable Care Act. But HHS has turned that into 429 pages of new regulations."*

Six pages from a recent bill comprising 907 pages spawned 429 pages of new regulations that were not voted on by Congress. That is 71 pages of regulation for every page of law, written and implemented by unelected bureaucrats who have personal, financial incentives to grow the size and scope of government, and who are shielded in Washington, D.C., from the economic damage they unleash with their regulations in the rest of the country.

John Stossel of Fox News reported that the U.S. federal government issued over 70,000 pages of regulations in 2009 alone. Many of those regulations contain financial penalties, and some even provide for criminal penalties.

What is the true cost of all this regulation? Freedom and independence. The notion of taking care of ourselves, making our own decisions, and looking out for our own families is considered outdated by an arrogant central government. Those of us who are average Americans just want to be left alone, but the politicians have decided that we are incapable of looking after ourselves.

WHAT DO THE TEA PARTY PATRIOTS PROPOSE?

THE CONGRESSIONAL REVIEW ACT
Right now, countless rules can be foisted upon America's most productive citizens, by unelected government "czars" and unaccountable bureaucrats, with little or no oversight. Under the Congressional Review Act (CRA), major rules must be submitted to both houses of Congress and the Government Accountability Office (GAO) before

*http://www.usnews.com/news/washington-whispers/articles/2011/04/07/6-pages-of
-obamacare-equals-429-pages-of-regulations.

they can take effect. The GAO defines a *major rule* as "one that has resulted in or is likely to result in (1) an annual effect on the economy of $100 million or more; (2) a major increase in costs or prices for consumers, individual industries, federal, state, or local government agencies, or geographic regions; or (3) significant adverse effects on competition, employment, investment, productivity, or innovation, or on the ability of United States–based enterprises to compete with foreign-based enterprises in domestic and export markets."

The Congressional Review Act is a potentially powerful tool to rein in out-of-control regulatory agencies. But Congress is unlikely to take this aggressive action without constant pressure from patriots across the country. It is far too easy for Congress to pass the laws, and for the bureaucracies to increase their numbers, power, and budgets, with a never-ending stream of restrictions. It is up to us to force Congress to use the CRA to prevent the imposition of regulatory tyranny.

RETURN THE GOVERNMENT TO THE FIRST FOUR ORIGINAL DEPARTMENTS

Government has now grown far beyond anything ever imagined by the Founders in its intrusiveness, size, number of departments, and complexity. In 1789, the federal government consisted of only three cabinet-level departments: State, Treasury, and War (today called Defense). In addition, the chief legal authority under the executive branch was a cabinet member as of 1789, though the Department of Justice itself wasn't established until 1870.

Today, there are fourteen cabinet-level departments, each of which has innumerable agencies, bureaus, programs, and administrators. The system has become a vast bureaucratic maze. Many Tea Partiers propose abolishing *all* cabinet-level departments of the U.S. government other than State, Treasury, Defense, and Justice. Such a reorganization would have to take place over several years but would dramatically reduce the federal government.

Our two prime targets for immediate elimination are the Departments of Energy and Education. These are two recently added departments, which have been dismal failures as we will demonstrate in the following pages. Doing away with them would save hundreds of billions of dollars and vastly improve the lives of the majority of American citizens.

The Department of Energy was created in 1977 by President Jimmy Carter after the first Middle East oil crisis. The majority of Americans still support Carter's goal of energy independence, but the department he started has not done anything to achieve it. In the 1970s, 36.1 percent of America's oil came from foreign sources. In the 1980s, after the Department of Energy was fully staffed, the percentage of American oil that came from foreign sources went up to 43.6 percent. In the 1990s, it went up to 49.8 percent. And by May 2011, that number was up to 61 percent.

What about oil prices? When the Department of Energy was created, oil cost $14.40 a barrel. It now regularly exceeds $100 a barrel. Even adjusted for inflation, oil is more than twice as expensive today as it was before we had a U.S. Department of Energy. While basic economics may suggest that the rise in the price of oil is a direct result of a reduction in supply, the amount of recoverable oil has actually *increased* in the past thirty years, due to advances in technology. In 1970, the world's proven oil reserves were about 612 billion barrels. By 2006, we had already pumped more than that amount, and the proven reserves stood at more than a trillion barrels.*

As for encouraging domestic production, the department's record is dismal, particularly if we hold it accountable for all the new experimental energy sources that have not yet been shown to work. But let's just check in on the domestic energy source that has been proved successful: nuclear power.

Well before the Department of Energy was even established, construction had begun on the most recent American nuclear plant. Since then . . . nothing, although the department's budget grew from $10.4 billion in 1977 to $26.4 billion in fiscal year 2010, with roughly a 76 percent increase in just the past decade—the same decade in which energy prices skyrocketed, and America became more dependent on foreign oil.

* http://www.washingtonpost.com/wp-dyn/content/article/2009/11/20/AR2009112002619
.html.

The government has had years to deliver . . . nothing. Worse, it has put America significantly farther behind than it was in 1977 and wasted billions of taxpayer dollars while those same taxpayers were paying more for energy. It is time to unleash the power of the free market, and the ingenuity and hard work of the American people, to get the job done.

Writing for the Heritage Foundation, Nicolas Loris, policy analyst at the Thomas A. Roe Institute for Economic Policy Studies, states:

> The reality is that when it comes to energy policy, the free market works. Indeed, the business environment for energy is robust despite seemingly endless forays by policymakers and bureaucrats into the energy industry. But those attempts to control energy markets do have an effect: They result in higher prices, fewer available energy sources, reduced competition, and stifled innovation . . .
>
> By attempting to force government-developed technologies into the market, the government diminishes the role of the entrepreneur and crowds out private-sector investment . . . Thus, almost without exception, it fails in some way.*

Congress should immediately eliminate any Department of Energy function that does not support a critical national interest unmet by the private sector. This could very well result in the elimination of the entire department. Regulation of the nuclear industry and other areas of critical national interest could be handled by much smaller, more efficient, scaled-down entities.

The Department of Education is another example of bureaucracy gone mad. According to the National Center for Education Statistics, its original budget, in 1980, was $13.1 billion (adjusted for 2007 dollars) and it employed a mere 450 people. By 2000 the cost had increased to $34.1 billion, and by 2007 it was up to $73 billion. The president's 2012 budget request for the Department of Education is $77.4 billion. The

---

* http://www.heritage.org/Research/Reports/2011/04/Department-of-Energy-Spending
  -Cuts-A-Guide-to-Trimming-President-Obamas-2012-Budget-Request.

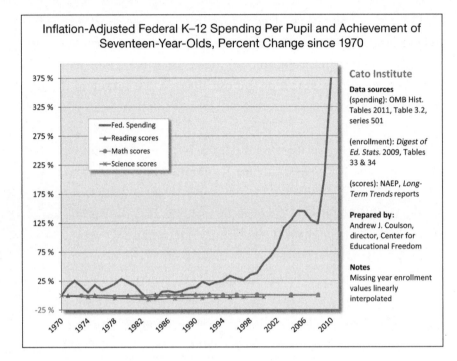

Inflation-Adjusted Federal K–12 Spending Per Pupil and Achievement of Seventeen-Year-Olds, Percent Change since 1970

Cato Institute

Data sources
(spending): OMB Hist. Tables 2011, Table 3.2, series 501

(enrollment): *Digest of Ed. Stats.* 2009, Tables 33 & 34

(scores): NAEP, *Long-Term Trends* reports

Prepared by:
Andrew J. Coulson, director, Center for Educational Freedom

Notes
Missing year enrollment values linearly interpolated

department's staff is now approximately five thousand. So what have all these employees, and all this spending, given us in terms of results?

As the chart above clearly shows, despite spending more and more money, test scores have not improved. Clearly we cannot improve educational quality simply by increasing spending.

> *I hope it doesn't have one.*
>
> —1981 note by RONALD REAGAN in the margin of a letter from a congressman, asking for a meeting to discuss the future of the Department of Education

Tea Partiers understand that federal government involvement in education is more than a colossal waste; it is a damaging influence on generations of children. Chapter 6 of this book lays out a detailed accounting of what is wrong with America's public education system, and chapter 7 contains our detailed analysis and recommendations on how to improve it.

But for the purposes of economic matters, the short answer is: disband the Department of Education and put that money toward actually educating our children, or, better, give it back to parents so they can choose the education options that are best for their children.

MONETARY POLICY

I believe that banking institutions are more danger-ous to our liberties than standing armies. Already they have raised up a monied aristocracy that has set the government at defiance. The issuing power (of money) should be taken away from the banks and restored to the people to whom it properly belongs.

—THOMAS JEFFERSON

Every effort has been made by the Fed to conceal its power but the truth is, the Fed has usurped the government. It controls everything here and it controls all our foreign relations. It makes and breaks governments at will.

—CONGRESSMAN LOUIS T. MCFADDEN, 1933, chairman, Banking and Currency Committee

AUDIT OF THE FEDERAL RESERVE

The U.S. Federal Reserve System (aka *the Fed*) describes itself as "the central bank of the United States" with a mandate to "provide the nation with a safer, more flexible, and more stable monetary and financial system" and notes, in a flourish of understatement, "Over the years, its role in banking and the economy has expanded."

Yes. It has.

Its duties today, according to its own documentation, are to regulate banking institutions, author and control the nation's monetary policy, and create stability in the financial system. It also provides a variety of services to depository institutions, the U.S. government, and a multitude of international entities.

Lately, the Fed's main job has been to print money, which has debased U.S. currency, driven up inflation, and caused the world to seriously reconsider decoupling itself from the U.S. dollar. And the Fed has been doing all this beyond the reach of the people's representatives. The Fed has consistently taken the position that it operates outside the supervisory purview of both the legislative and executive branches. However, its authority is granted by the U.S. Congress, and it is supposed to be subject to congressional oversight. But the Fed is strenuously resistant to an audit of its operations, stating that a true accounting would restrict its independence and autonomy.

Stated another way: the entity that controls our money supply, sets our interest rates, and creates inflation or deflation at its whim doesn't even have to comply with the basic principles of accounting oversight that any company has to observe to be listed on a stock exchange. Most people find this fact stunning. And 75 percent of Americans, according to a 2009 Rasmussen poll, want the Fed audited. We, the Tea Party Patriots, agree with 75 percent of Americans: the time to audit the Fed is now.

OUT-OF-CONTROL SPENDING

The multiplication of public offices, increase of expense beyond income, growth and entailment of a public debt, are indications soliciting the employment of the pruning knife.

—THOMAS JEFFERSON,
letter to Spencer Roane, March 9, 1821

Government is like a baby. An alimentary canal with a big appetite at one end and no sense of responsibility at the other.

—RONALD REAGAN

All levels of government have grown in size and scope. Even in the time of Thomas Jefferson, way back in 1821, people were concerned about national debt. And today we keep going deeper and deeper into a black hole of government debt.

The 2012 budget offered by President Obama in January 2011 showed a projected $1.6 trillion deficit for fiscal 2011. The current debt owed by the U.S. government is $14.7 trillion (but will be substantially more by the time this book is in print). That comes out to over $47,000 per citizen. That's right, every child born in America today will face a $47,000 debt. And that's just at the federal level. If you live in a fiscally irresponsible state like California or New Jersey, every baby will be burdened by another $10,000. For those children born in New York, add an extra $15,000. (If you have the stomach for it, you can watch the debt grow minute by minute at http://www.usdebtclock.org.) That is the gift our politicians are bequeathing to future generations.

So what can we do? The answer is simple. Stop overspending. We don't have a revenue problem; we have a spending problem. Spending, whether politicians call it *discretionary* or *mandatory*, is really *all* discretionary. Every law can be repealed or amended, and every program can be revised or scrapped. The question is not really whether something can be done; the question is whether our politicians have the political will to act.

We have to accept some basic facts about America's deficit before we can hold any reasonable discussion:

- The tax base is too small to solve the problem.
- Discretionary spending is too small to solve the problem.
- Mandatory entitlement programs are the *real* problem.

The scale of the problem can be assessed like this:

- Even if *all* discretionary spending were cut 50 percent, there would still be a $1-trillion deficit in 2011.
- Even if *all* current taxes were increased by 50 percent, there would still be a $1-trillion deficit in 2011.

When you examine both concepts, it becomes clear that "mandatory" programs are the real problem.

Some lawmakers want to raise individual income taxes on the "wealthy" to reduce the federal deficit. But aside from the fact that Tea Party members are almost universally opposed to tax increases, what would such an increase accomplish?

The projected federal deficit in the 2012 budget is $1.1 trillion. This is significantly lower than the deficit of 2011, which the 2012 budget estimates will wind up as $1.6 trillion. Let us assume that the progressive/liberal dream could be accomplished with a snap of the fingers, and income taxes on everyone doubled without affecting the economy. Even if the entire individual income tax were doubled, the projected deficit could not be bridged.

Obviously, the damage to the economy would be catastrophic. Consumer spending would plummet, businesses would collapse, unemployment would skyrocket, and the economy would plunge into chaos. Of course, assumptions about tax revenues would have to be revised, because so many people would be out of work. So if we can't double everyone's income taxes, how about just raising them on the rich?

If we use 2008 IRS data, this would roughly be the result: In 2008, the top 1 percent of all earners in America (those making more than about $380,000 a year) paid approximately 38 percent of all individual income taxes. This tax revenue to the federal government was $392 billion. So if taxes on these individuals were doubled, only $400 billion in new revenue might be raised. With a $1.6-trillion deficit, this is clearly not enough to solve the deficit problem, let alone pay off our existing debt.

When we take it down to the next level, the top 5 percent of all income earners (those making about $159,000 a year or more) are responsible for the payment of 59 percent of income taxes. This results in revenues of about $600 billion. Many of those people, while financially well off, certainly aren't hugely wealthy. However, even if taxes on these "rich fat-cats" were doubled, an additional $600 billion could be raised. Still not enough to make a dent in that $1.6-trillion deficit.